CELLO

THE G. SCHIRMER CELLO ANTHOLOGY

12 Works from the 20th Century

See Cello/Piano Score for Notes on the Music

ISBN 978-1-4803-6306-9

ED 4550

G. SCHIRMER, *Inc.*

Distributed By

7777 W. Bluemound Rd. P.O. Box 13819 Milwaukee, WI 53213

www.musicsalesclassical.com
www.halleonard.com

CONTENTS

Works for Cello and Piano

Samuel Barber
4 ADAGIO
second movement from Sonata, Op. 6

Ernest Bloch
6 MODERATO
first movement from *Voice in the Wilderness*

Carlos Chávez
7 MADRIGAL

Henry Cowell
9 FOUR DECLAMATIONS WITH RETURN

Bohuslav Martinů
12 LARGO
second movement from Sonata No. 2

Robert Xavier Rodríguez
22 LULL-A-BEAR
from *Ursa*

Joan Tower
20 TRÈS LENT
(Hommage à Messiaen)

Works for Solo Cello

John Corigliano
8 FANCY ON A BACH AIR

Ezra Laderman
10 SECOND MOVEMENT
from Partita for Solo Cello
(Meditations on Isaiah)

Robert Muczynski
14 GALLERY
Suite for unaccompanied Cello

Bright Sheng
18 PASTORAL BALLADE
sixth movement from *Seven Tunes Heard in China*

Augusta Read Thomas
24 SPRING SONG*

** Note that this part may be carefully cut from the book*

Adagio

second movement from Sonata, Op. 6

Samuel Barber
(1910–1981)
Composed in 1932

cresc. poco a poco
Ia
35
f
accel.
41
ff a tempo
f
pizz.
p
2
48
di nuovo Adagio
arco
p mf
molto espress.
poco rit.
mp a tempo
f
55
ff

dim. poco a poco
rit.
p

Moderato

first movement from *Voice in the Wilderness*

Ernest Bloch
(1880–1959)
Composed in 1936

* In original piece, there is an *attacca* here.

Madrigal

Edited by Max Lifchitz

Carlos Chávez
(1899–1978)
Composed in 1921

Fancy on a Bach Air

John Corigliano
(b. 1938)
Composed in 1996

for Seymour Barab & William Masselos

Four Declamations with Return

Henry Cowell
(1897–1965)
Composed in 1949

Second Movement

from Partita for Solo Cello (Meditations on Isaiah)

Ezra Laderman
(b. 1924)
Composed in 1971

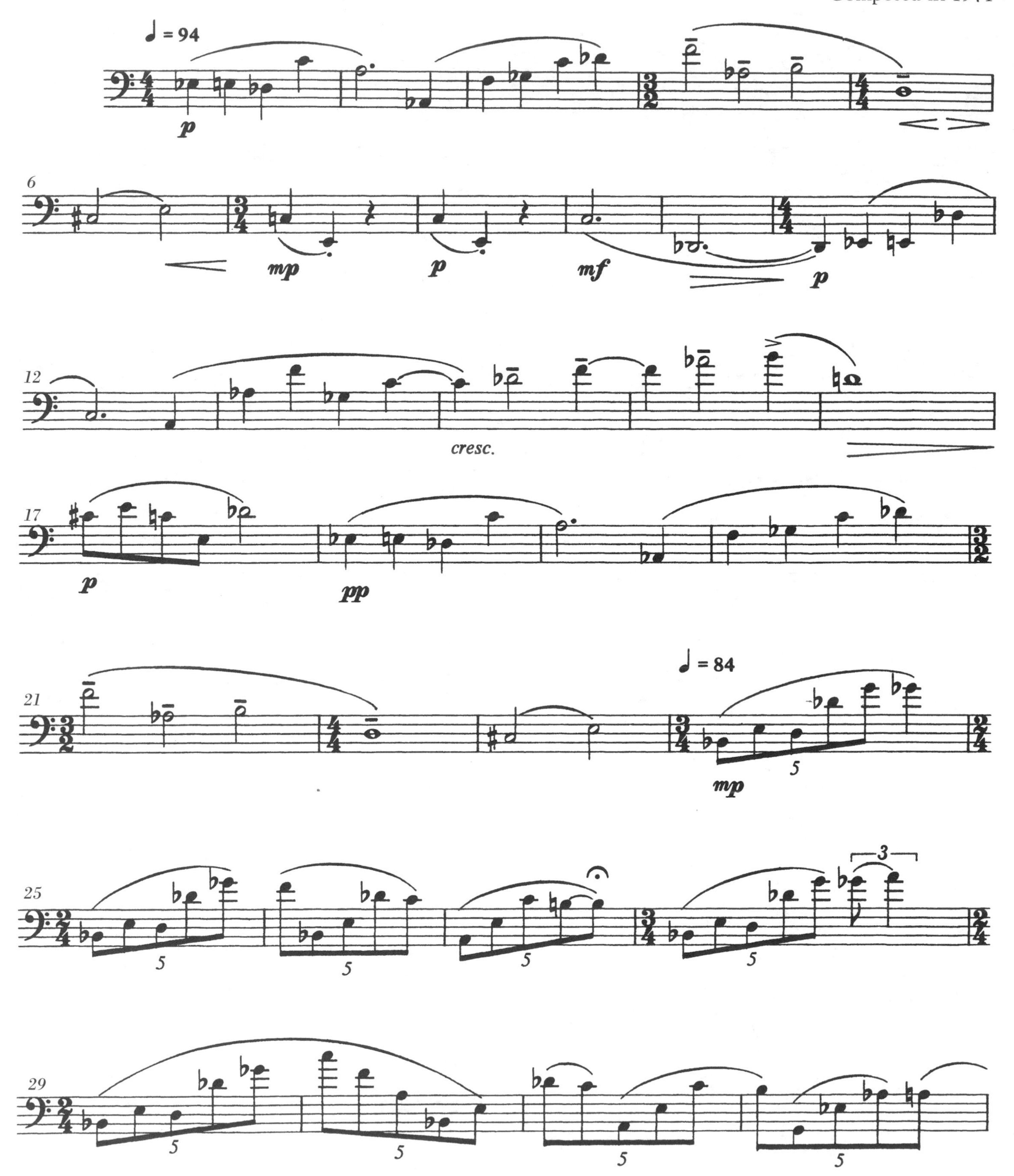

33
5
5
5

ritard.
= 94
36
3
3
3
ppp

39

43
p

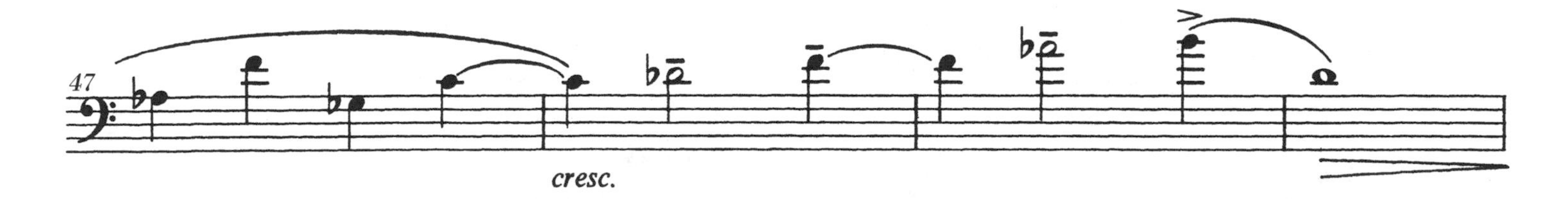
47
cresc.

51
p
pp
cresc.

55
f
f

59
mf
mp
p
pp

Largo

second movement from Sonata No. 2

Cello part edited and fingered
by Lucien Laporte Kirsch

Bohuslav Martinů
(1890–1959)
Composed in 1941

F
molto f
G
molto f
sul G
H
I
suivez
p dolce
poco
pp

Gallery

Suite for unaccompanied Cello

Edited by
Gordon Epperson

Robert Muczynski
(1929–2010)

Composed in 1971

4. Shanty

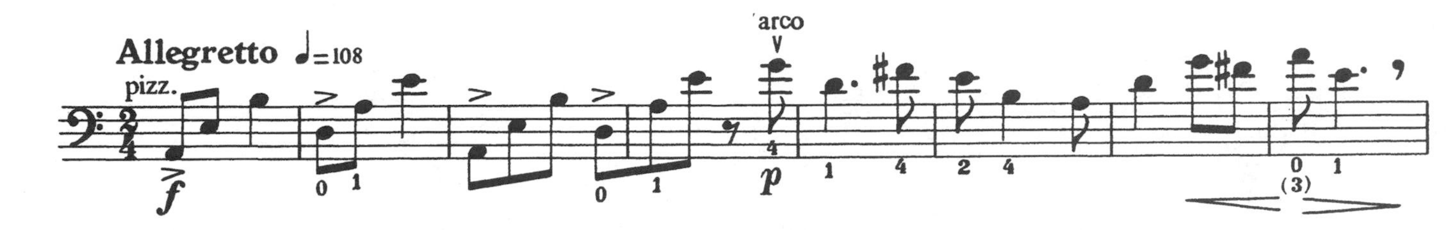
Allegretto ♩=108
pizz.
arco

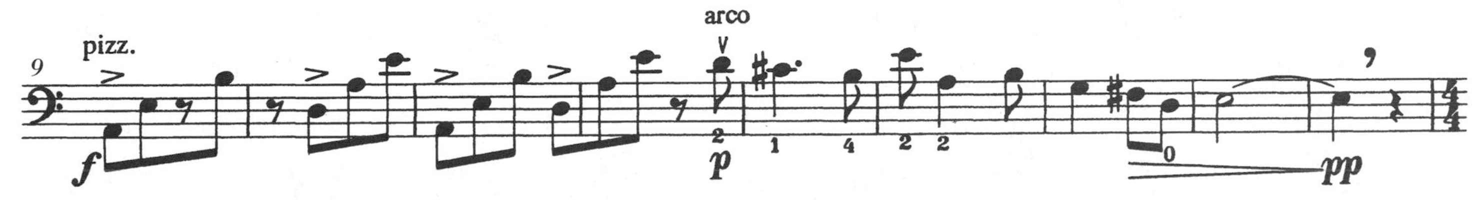
9
pizz.
arco

Allegro ♩=126
18
f marc.
grazioso

23
allarg.
a tempo
f marc.

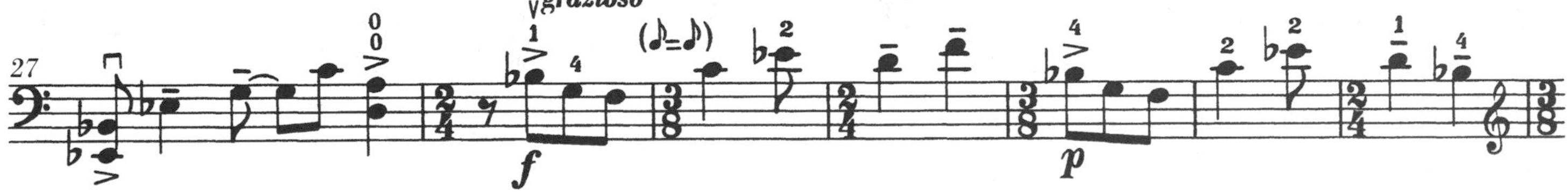
27
grazioso

34

41

46
più f

52
allarg.
marc.

5. Winter Houses
Andante
p sost.
pizz. (lightly accented)
a tempo
poco rit.
(short)
arco
rit.
attacca
6. Ice Glare
Poco più mosso
pizz.
(mysteriously)
sost.
Meno mosso
7. Black Iron
Allegro
(well-accented)
marc.
cresc.

8. September Light

9. End of the Day

Moderato ♩=72

p sost.

attacca

Adagio ♩=72

p espress., sost.

rit.

+(L.H. pizz.)

Pastoral Ballade
sixth movement from Seven Tunes Heard in China
Bright Sheng
(b. 1955)
Composed in 1995
Edited by Yo-Yo Ma
♩ = 54
mf warmly espr., wide vib.
III
sul D
poco
poco meno mosso (♩ = 50)
poco tasto
pp dolce
a tempo
ord.
poco meno mosso
pp poco tasto
accel. al
al
ord.
poco meno mosso
poco tasto
pp sub.
accel. al
a tempo
molto
♩ = 72

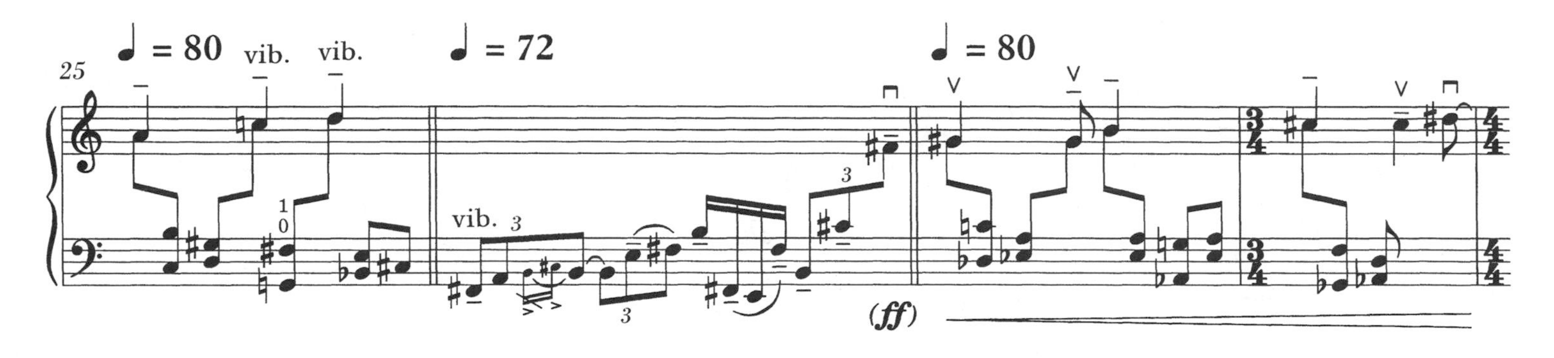
25
♩ = 80
vib.
vib.
♩ = 72
♩ = 80
vib.
(ff)

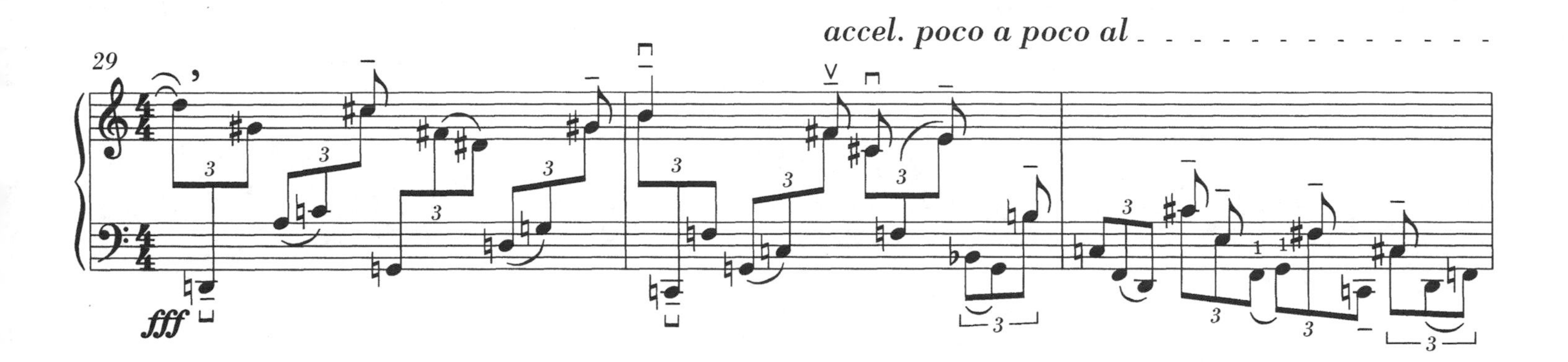
29
accel. poco a poco al
fff

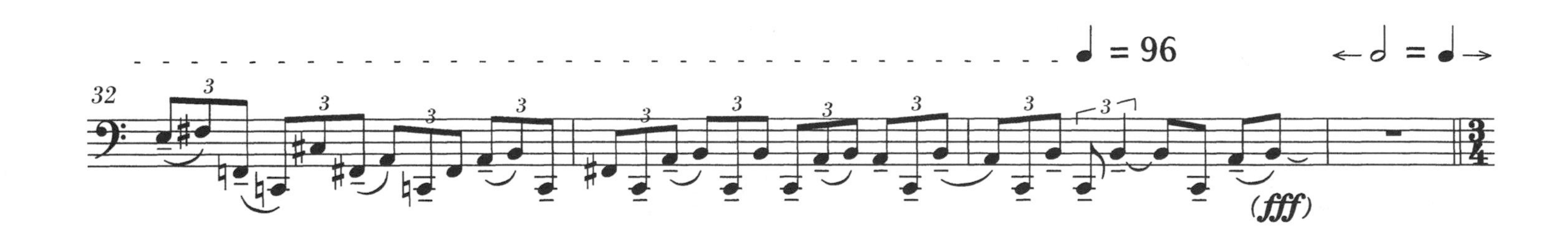
32
♩ = 96
(fff)

𝅗𝅥 = ♩ = 48
36
poco
tasto
III II
ppp sempre

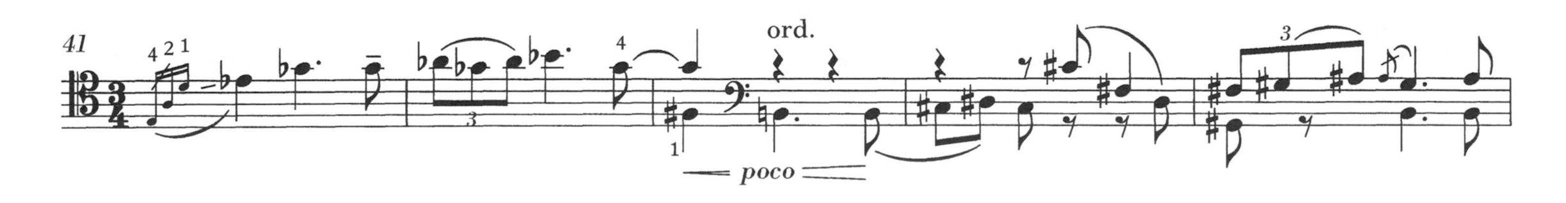
41
ord.
poco

46
sul D
poco

to Andre Emelianoff

Très Lent
(Hommage à Messiaen)

Joan Tower
(b. 1938)
Composed in 1994

26
3
cresc.

28
f
mp
p dolce (warmer)

31
3
ppp lontano
3

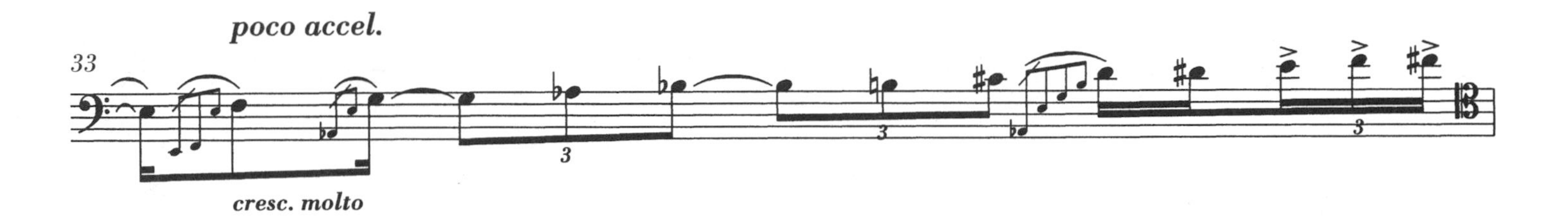
poco accel.
33
cresc. molto
3
3
3

Poco più mosso ♪ = ca. 48 (♪ = ca. 96)
34
sim.
ff appassionata
3
3
3
3
3
3
3

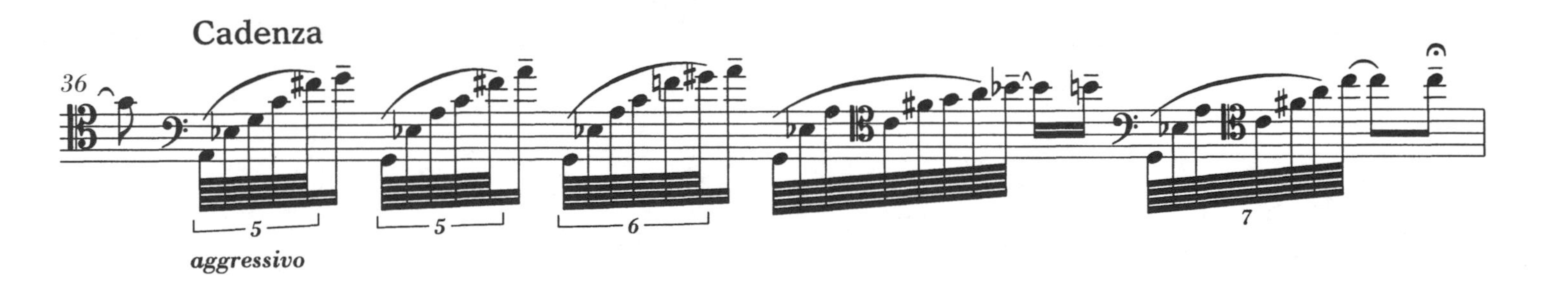
Cadenza
36
5
5
6
7
aggressivo

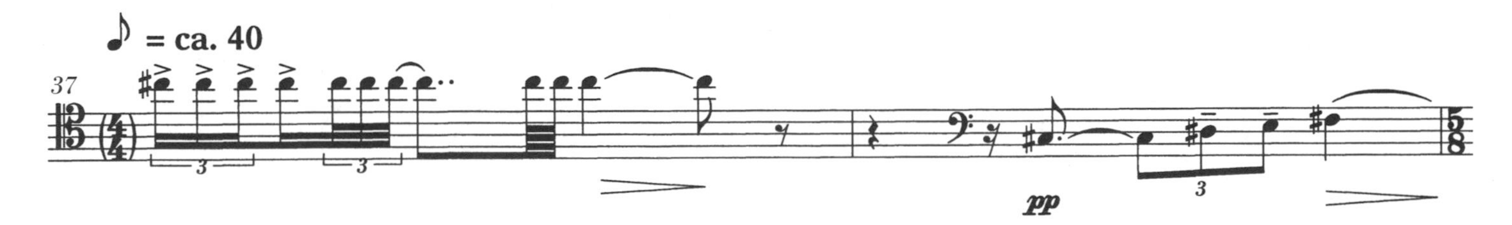
♪ = ca. 40
37
3
3
3
pp

rit.
Meno mosso
39
3
3
3
3
3
ppp
p
dim.
pp
cresc.
pp
dim.

Lull-A-Bear

from *Ursa*

Robert Xavier Rodríguez
(b. 1946)
Composed in 1994

for Scott Kluksdahl

Spring Song

Augusta Read Thomas
(b. 1964)
Composed in 1995

*Play mm. 16–33 as one long phrase, with subphrases of mm. 16–24, 25–27, 28–30, 31, and 32.
Note that this part may be carefully cut from book.

Molto intenso, bell–like ♩ = 104–112
33
(ff sempre)
37
rit.
Molto rubato ♩ = 92
42
f
ff cant.
rit.
lunga
♩ = 80
f
46
ff molto legato
rit.
f
ff
♩ = 58
molto rubato
52
p
cant.
mp
pp
p
55
sul D
mf
pp sotto voce,
bell–like, echo
♩ = 96
mf
playful
ff
sul D,
al punta
mf < f
sul G,
spiccato
58
mf
ff
p sotto voce
(♩ = 96)
ff sempre
62
spicc.

65
mp
secco
f
p sub.
f
6
p sub.
f
68
ff
5
mf sub.
ff
mp
secco
f
freely
p sub.
mf
ff
71
freely
f
ff
5
f
Bold and broad ♩ = 86
ff molto cant.
73
3
3
75
accel.
mf sub., secco
3
3
ff
♩ = 112
78
ff sempre
81
♩ = 84
3
f
3
ff
85
3
88
rit.
Molto rubato ♩ = 60
f
(f)
5
mp
mf
Molto cantabile ♩ = 52
lunga
92
7:6
p
sentimental, dolce
mp
pp
mp
pp
molto espr.,
like a sigh